CAREERS *in Your Community*™

WORKING

in

HEALTH SERVICES

Jessica Shaw

Rosen
YA™
New York

Published in 2019 by The Rosen Publishing Group, Inc.
29 East 21st Street, New York, NY 10010

First Edition

Library of Congress Cataloging-in-Publication Data

Names: Shaw, Jessica, 1972– author.
Title: Working in health services / Jessica Shaw.
Description: New York : Rosen YA, 2019 | Series: Careers in your community | Audience: Grades 7–12. | Includes bibliographical references and index.
Identifiers: LCCN 2018010327| ISBN 9781499467307 (library bound) | ISBN 9781499467383 (pbk.)
Subjects: LCSH: Medicine—Vocational guidance—Juvenile literature. | Medical sciences—Vocational guidance—Juvenile literature. | Medical personnel—Juvenile literature.
Classification: LCC R690 .S4595 2018 | DDC 610.69023—dc23
LC record available at https://lccn.loc.gov/2018010327

Manufactured in the United States of America

Contents

Introduction

The ancient Egyptians practiced medicine as early as 3100 BCE. Their methods included magic spells and charms, crude surgical techniques, and the use of herbs, oils, and other plant-derived substances. The ancient Egyptians weren't the first to try their hands at health care, however. Scientists believe that Neanderthals may have used primitive health care remedies more than sixty thousand years ago.

Between 800 BCE and 400 CE the ancient Greeks forged ahead with what would become the foundation of modern scientific medicine. The Greek physician Hippocrates is known as the "Father of Modern Medicine." He paved the way, establishing medicine as a serious profession when he founded the Hippocratic School of Medicine. Hippocrates also created the Hippocratic oath, which is a vow that students take upon completion of requirements for their job in health care or upon graduation from medical school. The vow is a promise that they will practice medicine in an ethical and honest manner. The ancient Romans made significant contributions to medicine, inventing many surgical instruments and performing the first cataract surgeries.

From 400 to 1300 CE, Islamic physicians continued to build on medical knowledge. They expanded medicine

HIPOCRATI COO

Hippocrates made many significant contributions to the field of medicine but is best known for the oath that bears his name.

into the fields of child development and psychotherapy. In 1628, an English physician named William Harvey made an important discovery about blood circulation, laying the foundation for an in-depth understanding of the entire circulatory system.

In Colonial America, Benjamin Franklin and Dr. Thomas Bond founded the first hospital, Pennsylvania Hospital, in 1751. At the time, its purpose was to provide housing and medical services to the poor, but Pennsylvania Hospital still functions today as a private hospital. Soon after the hospital's founding, the first medical school in the colonies was founded in 1765 in what is now Pennsylvania.

In 1847 the American Medical Association (AMA) was founded. Members embarked on a mission to establish medical standards of care and ethical guidelines and to promote the scientific advancement of health care. By 1910, membership in the AMA had grown to seventy thousand. This period of time became known as the start of organized medicine. Throughout the coming decades, surgeries became commonplace, new medicines and treatments were developed, and many more schools specifically devoted to the education of health service professionals were established.

The number of jobs in health services has risen steadily since the era of organized medicine began. The manufacturing and retail industries in the United States have traditionally been the leaders when it comes to number of employees in the workforce. However, in 2017, for the first time ever, the health care industry topped both manufacturing and retail to become the largest source of jobs in the United States.

Thanks to advancements in medical technologies and improvements in training, education, and methodologies, people are living longer lives. Many medical conditions that were previously terminal have become treatable. Simply put, there are more people to keep well than ever before. In addition, government-backed programs such as Medicare and Medicaid pump hundreds of billions of dollars into the industry to cover health costs for those in need, creating a high demand for more and more health care employees.

CHAPTER One

Physicians and Dentists: Caring for Communities

f asked to name professions in health care, many people would think of doctors and dentists immediately. Physicians (commonly referred to as doctors) and

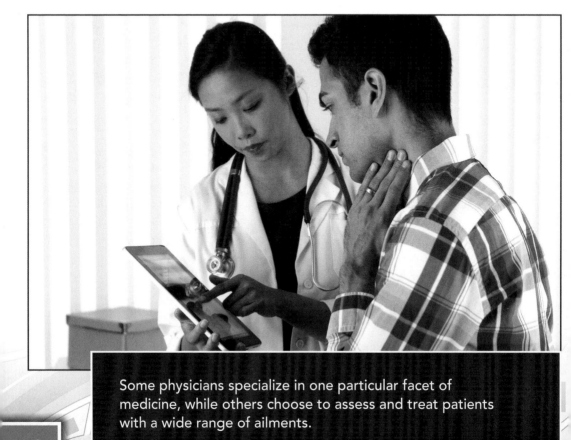

Some physicians specialize in one particular facet of medicine, while others choose to assess and treat patients with a wide range of ailments.

dentists are, after all, two health care professionals that individuals see on a fairly regular basis throughout their lives. Oral care and overall health care are basic needs, and those who become doctors or dentists will be helping countless patients live longer, healthier lives.

The Path to Becoming a Physician

The road to becoming a physician is not a quick or easy one. Students pursuing careers as physicians should have a strong academic focus, beginning in high school, with an emphasis on advanced science and math classes. Often, students can take dual credit college classes while still in high school, which is a great opportunity to take additional science and math courses.

In college, most students pursuing a career in medicine choose majors such as premed, science, psychology, or math. After completing the requirements for a bachelor's degree, the next step is taking the MCAT (Medical College Admission Test) and applying to medical school. Medical schools are highly selective and applicants need to have earned a high GPA in their undergraduate course work to gain admission.

The first two years of medical school are packed with intensive classroom and clinical study of the human body and all of its complex systems. During the third and fourth years of medical school, students begin completing supervised rotations, which means students try out many different medical specialties and give input on diagnosis and treatment of patients.

After earning an MD (doctor of medicine) degree, students must choose a specialty and begin their residency in a hospital or other clinical setting. Residencies typically last three to four years. Upon completion of a residency, the last step is passing the United States Medical Licensing Examination (USMLE). At that point, a medical license is granted, allowing the doctor to legally practice medicine in the United States.

Physicians: Specialties, Skills, and Responsibilities

There are a multitude of specialties for physicians. Job settings, salaries, and specific day-to-day responsibilities vary depending on the type of specialty, but generally speaking, all physicians examine patients and diagnose illnesses or injuries of some type. They provide treatment for the condition and give patients medical advice to help them achieve optimal health. Medical doctors need to be aware of their patients' medical histories to provide them with the best care, and this means a great deal of time is spent on reviewing charts and talking with patients. Doctors must determine which, if any, laboratory tests are needed and whether or not a patient needs to be referred to a doctor in another specialty area. Effective communication with patients and their loved ones is essential, as they may have a great many questions about their diagnosis, test results, or medical treatment.

Pediatricians are doctors who specialize in the medical care and treatment of children. This means they have completed their residency in pediatrics and have a special interest in making sure children stay healthy and reach the appropriate growth and development markers. Obstetricians are the physicians who welcome babies into

In addition to their specialized medical training to treat children, pediatricians must also be especially good at interacting with children and putting them at ease.

the world and help mothers stay healthy during and after pregnancy. Neurologists diagnose and treat conditions involving the central and peripheral nervous systems. Emergency medicine doctors specialize in treating patients who come to emergency rooms with potentially life-threatening illnesses or injuries. Surgeons are physicians who have been trained to perform surgeries. There are dozens of specialty areas, and these are just a few of the most common. There are also areas of subspecialty within the specialty areas, so students who want to become doctors have an impressive and interesting list to choose from when it's time to begin their residencies.

The education and training required to become a physician is daunting, but physicians' salaries are among the highest of all occupations. Prospective physicians have a variety of choices in specialty and can look forward

IHS: HEALTH PROFESSIONALS SERVING NATIVE AMERICAN COMMUNITIES

The Indian Health Service (IHS) is a federal health program for American Indians and Alaska Natives. It operates under the umbrella of the Department of Health and Human Services, providing free health services to approximately 2.2 million members of federally recognized tribes across thirty-six states. In exchange for a minimum two-year agreement to provide service in IHS health facilities, physicians and dentists can take advantage of the IHS Loan Repayment Program (LRP). The LRP helps participants repay their health profession education loans for as long as they continue providing services in IHS facilities. Participants may choose to renew their contract each year, and for each year of service the LRP will continue to contribute to repayment of eligible loans, up to $40,000. Medical and dental schools are expensive institutions, and working for the IHS is one way to help pay off student loans while also helping an underserved population.

to a challenging and rewarding career. According to the Bureau of Labor Statistics (BLS), the number of physician jobs is expected to grow at a faster-than-average rate of 13 percent between 2016 and 2026. This will amount to more than ninety thousand new jobs.

The Path to Becoming a Dentist

Like physicians, dentists also face a rigorous academic path. Focusing on science and math courses is important, along with a solid foundation in all of the core classes. Classes such as biology, algebra, and chemistry are especially important. Being academically driven is essential, as the field of dentistry is competitive and success will depend, to a large degree, on performance in coursework and exams. Any hobby or activity that keeps the hands and fingers in shape is a good idea, since manual dexterity is crucial to dentistry. Some high schools offer internships or job shadow programs. If that type of program is available, getting an early look at what dentistry is like can help students decide if dentistry is what they want to do.

Some colleges offer a predentistry major. If that's not available, students will often choose to major in some area of science, since most dental schools require applicants to have completed many hours of science courses. Maintaining a high GPA in college is important, as are any volunteering or job shadowing experiences in the field of dentistry. Students will need to take the Dental Admissions Test (DAT) before applying to an American Dental Association (ADA) accredited dental school.

Like medical school, dental school takes four years to complete. Dental students take advanced courses in biology, anatomy, pharmacology, and microbiology, just to name a few. They learn about different facets of dentistry such as periodontics, orthodontics, pediatric dentistry, and oral surgery. They also complete clinical rotations that give them the chance to observe dentists and work with patients. Upon completion of dental school, students earn either a doctor of dental surgery (DDS) or doctor of medicine in dentistry (DMD), depending on the program they completed.

Once the education requirements are out of the way, there are two final hurdles to gain licensure. First, candidates must pass both parts of the written National Board Dental Examinations. Next, candidates in most states must fulfill a clinical examination requirement. Individual states use regional testing agencies to administer the clinical examination. The few states that don't require a clinical examination instead require candidates to complete an accredited post-graduate dental education program of at least one year in length.

Dentists at Work

Dentistry is a rewarding profession that touches lives and transforms smiles. Dentists diagnose and treat infections, diseases, injuries, and structural problems in the mouth. They perform surgical procedures when needed, including extractions, implants, and root canals. And, perhaps most importantly, they educate their patients about oral disease prevention and how to best care for their teeth at home, between professional cleanings. The field of dentistry has progressed by leaps and bounds in its use of technology. Lasers and computer-aided treatments are commonplace,

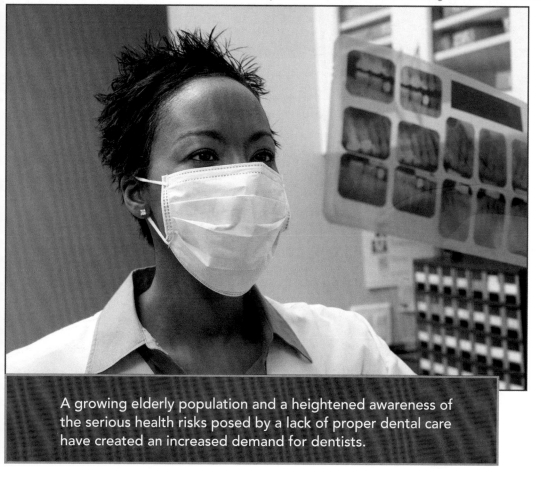

A growing elderly population and a heightened awareness of the serious health risks posed by a lack of proper dental care have created an increased demand for dentists.

and future dentists can look forward to utilizing cutting-edge equipment and methodologies in their practices.

The field of dentistry has been experiencing very rapid growth, creating a demand for more dentists. According to the BLS, there will be an additional 29,300 jobs added between 2016 and 2026. This equates to a much faster than average growth rate of 19 percent, making it a great time to pursue a dental career.

CHAPTER Two

Nursing and Medical Assisting: Vital Roles in Health Care

Nurses and medical assistants play a vital role in patient care. While waiting to see a doctor, patients will usually see a medical assistant or a nurse, and sometimes both. Those who pursue a career as a nurse or medical assistant can expect a career that is just as rewarding as it is challenging. There are several different types of nurses, and depending on the type of nurse a student wants to become, different degrees that correlate with each specific type.

A Career as an LPN-LVN

A licensed practicing nurse (LPN) and licensed vocational nurse (LVN) are the same thing. California and Texas use the LVN designation, while all other states use the LPN designation. Either way, this type of licensure can be obtained in two years or fewer and doesn't require a college degree. Before applying to nursing school, candidates must take the Test of Essential Academic Skills (TEAS). When researching nursing schools, it's important to choose one that is accredited by the state's board of nursing. After completing an LPN-LVN program,

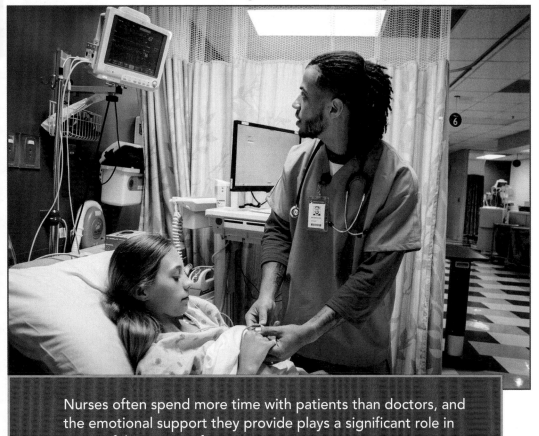

Nurses often spend more time with patients than doctors, and the emotional support they provide plays a significant role in successful outcomes for patients.

candidates must pass the National Council Licensure Examination (NCLEX) in order to practice.

LPN-LVNs perform a variety of functions, including maintaining records of patients' histories, cleaning medical equipment, measuring patients' vital signs, assisting with tests and procedures, providing dressing or bathing assistance, and updating doctors on a patient's status. They work in hospitals, nursing facilities, physicians' offices, and in-home health care. LPN-LVNs are expected to see a faster than average 12 percent growth in jobs from 2016 to 2026, according to the BLS. Some LPN-LVNs choose to continue their nursing education to take their career to the next level.

A Career as a Registered Nurse

For those who want to become a registered nurse (RN), a minimum of a two-year associate's degree is required. However, the majority of employers require their RNs to have a bachelor's of science in nursing (BSN) degree. After completion of all degree requirements, candidates need to pass the National Council Licensure Examination for Registered Nurses (NCLEX–RN) in order to practice as a RN.

In 2014, more than 2.7 million registered nurses were employed in the United States, with more than half of them working in hospitals. Others worked in doctors' offices, nursing facilities, schools, correctional facilities, and in-home health care. Registered nurses perform procedures and special tests, document treatment, evaluate diagnostic test results, provide care for emergency illnesses and injuries, administer medications, and start IVs. They are a source of information, support, and comfort for patients and their families and an integral part of successful health care.

Advanced Nursing Careers

Nurses who earn a master's degree are eligible to become advanced practice nurses (APNs), nurse practitioners (NPs), or certified registered nurse anesthetists (CRNAs). This level of nursing typically commands a higher salary as well as a higher degree of autonomy. APNs, NPs, and CRNAs often have areas of specialization, such as forensic nursing.

Forensic nursing is a fascinating area of specialty that involves collecting evidence, interacting directly with crime victims, and testifying to help convict those responsible for violent crimes.

Advanced practice nurses and other nurses with advanced training and degrees are in great demand. Nursing is one of the fastest-growing occupations, and the BLS predicts a much faster than average 31 percent growth in jobs between 2016 and 2026, which means there will be more than sixty-four thousand new jobs available. The United States has faced a nursing shortage for decades, and that shortage is expected to become even more dire, with a large aging population, an increase in chronic diseases that require more care, and a limited number of accredited schools to train nurses.

TIPS FOR HIGH SCHOOL STUDENTS INTERESTED IN NURSING

There is no shortage of fun distractions in high school that can pull students away from their studies. For those interested in a competitive field such as nursing, though, those distractions need to come in second to a strong focus on academics and preparation for a challenging career path. There are many steps high school students can take to set themselves up for success in a future nursing career.

- Put forth great effort in learning as much as possible in all math and science classes.
- Develop good test-taking strategies. There will be several important tests required along the path to becoming a nurse.
- Maintain a high GPA in high school, and take AP classes if possible.
- Take advantage of volunteer programs in hospitals or nursing homes to gain experience.
- Join the HOSA-Future Health Professionals program. This program is offered at the majority of high schools.

A Career as a Medical Assistant

Becoming a medical assistant is another great entry point to the health care field. Community colleges and trade schools offer training programs in medical assisting, and there are also a number of online programs available. A traditional college degree is not required and some programs for medical assisting take as few as six months to complete. The range is usually six months to two years for completion and entry into the workforce as a medical assistant.

Medical assistants are not required by law to have certification, but after completing a program and becoming a medical assistant, many choose to take the extra step of becoming certified or registered. Certified and registered are essentially the same things. Medical assistants can become certified medical assistants (CMA) through the American Association of Medical Assistants (AAMA), or they can go through the American Registry of Medical Assistants (ARMA) to become registered medical assistants. To be eligible, applicants must successfully complete a program in medical assisting, pass a certification exam, and participate in continuing education hours on an ongoing basis to recertify every five years. The benefit of either of these designations is a significantly higher salary, more job opportunities, and more opportunities for advancement.

There are three types of medical assistants: clinical, administrative, and traditional. Clinical medical assistants work closely with doctors and nurses. They administer medication and spend a great deal of time with patients as well as completing tasks such as medical instrument sterilization. Administrative medical assistants handle paperwork and other administrative tasks. They spend most of their workday at a desk rather than with patients. Traditional medical assistants cover both bases, working

The administrative duties handled by medical assistants are critical to ensuring doctors have the information they need to provide the very best care for patients.

with patients as well as completing administrative tasks. They have the advantage of gaining knowledge and experience in patient care as well as administrative functions.

As with nursing, medical assisting is experiencing a severe shortage of employees. The BLS predicts a growth rate of 29 percent between 2016 and 2026. This is much faster than average and will equate to 183,900 new jobs in medical assisting in that timeframe. With such a high demand for medical assistants, students who pursue this career are likely to have great job stability and many workplace options.

CHAPTER Three

Careers in Health and Wellness

Those who like the idea of a career that helps people improve their health and well-being might consider becoming a community health worker, dietitian, or nutritionist. Community health workers bridge the gap between members of a community and health professionals. They are health advocates for many groups of people who need help achieving health and wellness. Community health workers must be compassionate, knowledgeable, and have excellent communication skills. Similarly, dietitians and nutritionists work to promote health and wellness. They, too, must be excellent communicators who are committed to giving their clients the support and tools they need to be their healthiest selves.

Community Health Workers

Becoming a community health worker does not require a postsecondary education. Some community health workers have a two- or four-year degree, while

Health professionals trained in nutrition help people of all ages improve their eating habits to promote health and wellness.

others begin work right out of high school. Education requirements vary depending on the employer and the specific position applied for. Having a strong connection to and passion for helping a community is the most important quality for a community health worker.

Community health workers are employed in a variety of settings, including hospitals, rehabilitation centers, outpatient care centers, colleges, nonprofit organizations, community health centers, and family service offices. Community health workers often work with many different at-risk groups. Clients are often the elderly, those living in poverty, college students, at-risk kids, and people living with HIV.

Responsibilities and day-to-day tasks will vary for community health workers depending on where they work and the primary populations they serve. All community health workers provide social and emotional support, connect people with the resources they need to improve or maintain health and wellness, and provide information and education about health issues. Daily duties for a community health worker might include planning, promoting, and providing a service such as blood pressure screening, distributing health information door-to-door in the community, making phone calls to connect a community member with the help he or she needs, educating families with language or other barriers on the importance of vaccinations, serving as a liaison between a medical professional and patient, and explaining a treatment plan or home care instructions to a patient. Community health workers spend time researching specific health conditions, such as HIV, and educating members of the community about risks,

NUTRITIONIST OR DIETITIAN?

It's a common misconception that nutritionists and dietitians are the same thing. Although the professions are closely related, the level of training required creates a distinct difference. In order to become a registered dietitian, a rigorous academic and clinical education in nutrition is required, and candidates must pass an exam and complete continuing education hours. Nutritionists are not required to meet any specific academic requirements. However, the title of nutritionist is not legally regulated. Virtually anyone can call himself or herself a nutritionist. Nutritionists who want to make the most of their career can complete the requirements for becoming a dietitian as well.

prevention, treatments, and available resources. They help underserved populations receive increased access to health services and offer whole communities information and services that were previously lacking.

Between 2016 and 2026 the BLS estimates there will be a 16 percent growth rate in community health worker jobs. This means there will be an additional 19,200 jobs available during that timeframe. As with most jobs in health services, the outlook is favorable for job seekers in community health, with ample opportunities and a variety of work settings.

Dietitians and nutritionists encourage most patients to eat lean proteins, such as chicken or seafood, and a variety of fresh vegetables on a daily basis.

A Career as a Registered Dietitian Nutritionist

Becoming a registered dietitian nutritionist (RDN) requires completion of the specific set of college courses outlined by the Academy of Nutrition and Dietetics (AND). This can be done while completing a bachelor's degree or later, in graduate school. Upon completion of a bachelor's or master's degree, the candidate must complete a dietetic internship (DI). This involves researching the Accreditation Council for Education in Nutrition and Dietetics (ACEND) approved list of internship programs and applying to

WORKING FOR WIC

One option for nutritionists and dietitians is to work for the WIC program. WIC stands for Women, Infants, and Children. WIC is a supplemental nutrition program that is federally funded. States receive federal money to provide supplemental foods, nutrition education, and health and wellness support for low-income women during and after pregnancy, and to families with infants and children up to age five who are otherwise at risk of not receiving proper nutrition. WIC employees provide essential support, nutritional counseling, and health services to high-risk women, infants, and children. Nutritionists and dietitians at WIC play a vital role in promoting the health and wellness of low-income families.

one. The DI requires 1,200 hours of supervised practice and takes eight to twenty-four months to complete. Lastly, candidates must pass the Registered Dietitian Exam. There are also continuing education hours that are required on an ongoing basis to maintain registration.

Registered dietitian nutritionists work in a variety of settings, including hospitals, schools, long-term care facilities, community health facilities, government agencies, corporate nutrition programs, and within the food and nutrition industry. Depending upon where the RDN works, job tasks will vary. RDNs educate and counsel others on health, food, and nutrition. They assess the dietary needs of clients, develop meal plans, and provide support to clients striving to meet their health and wellness goals. Usually, they work with clients long term, until their health and wellness goals are met. RDNs may also promote good nutrition through community events and outreach programs.

The job outlook for registered dietitians is bright. BLS expects a 15 percent increase in jobs between 2016 and 2026. This means there will be 9,900 new job openings for those pursuing a career as a RDN.

A Career as a Nutritionist

Some nutritionists have no academic background or formal training to back up their job title. To be successful in this field requires more than just declaring a professional title. Nutritionists who want excellent job opportunities and a meaningful career need to first earn a bachelor's degree in a health-related field such as food science, nutrition, or biology. Some students choose to take their education one step further, earning a master's degree in a graduate nutrition program. Nutritionists who take the necessary steps to become licensed can expect to be at the top of their field. Nutritionist certification boards require applicants to have an advanced degree and some practical experience. Once those qualifications are met, they can take the certification exam. Nutritionists who pass this exam earn the title of certified nutrition specialist (CNS).

Nutritionists work in many settings, including schools, cafeterias, government agencies, nonprofits, hospitals, and nursing homes. Where a nutritionist is able to find employment depends on their level of education and

In order to increase the odds of maintaining healthy eating habits, many people need help learning how to properly prepare nutritious foods.

whether or not they are a CNS. Nutritionists are experts in food and nutrition, and as such, their primary objectives are to help clients achieve better health and wellness through their diets. They may plan menus, consult with clients, provide essential information on nutrition and health to individuals or groups, and provide support and motivation to clients with weight loss or other nutrition-related goals. Nutritionists are categorized with dietitians by the BLS, meaning the job outlook is the same—very good, especially for those willing to go above and beyond in their education.

CHAPTER Four

Health Care Technologists

Many health care professionals choose a career as a health care technologist. There are multiple areas of specialization to choose from and some require no more than two years of training before earning a paycheck. Health care technologists work in hospitals, outpatient surgical centers, clinical laboratories, imaging centers, and physicians' offices. There are a myriad of technologist jobs in health services, including surgical techs, radiologic techs, and clinical laboratory techs. The academic and training requirements are different for each type of technologist.

A Career as a Surgical Technologist

Those interested in a career as a surgical technologist typically enroll in programs offered by community and junior colleges, vocational schools, universities, or hospitals. Some certification programs take as few as twelve months to complete, while others are two-year programs that offer an associate's degree. Most surgical-tech programs require only a high school education for acceptance, but some require applicants to have successfully completed some classes in medical

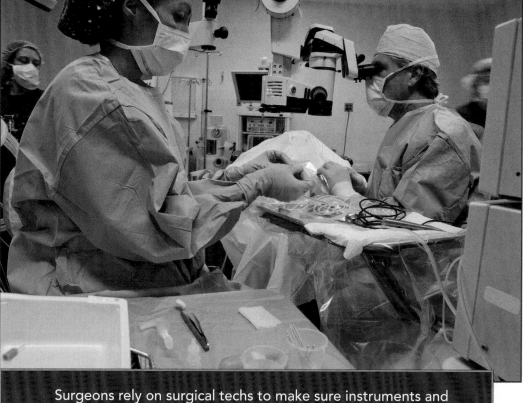

Surgeons rely on surgical techs to make sure instruments and equipment are properly sterilized and necessary supplies are on hand to keep everything running smoothly.

terminology and the sciences. Upon graduation from an accredited program, candidates are eligible to take the national surgical technology certification examination offered by the National Board of Surgical Technology and Surgical Assisting (NBSTSA).

A surgical technologist's primary function is assisting before, during, and after a surgical procedure. Surgical technologists are an important part of the operating room team, which typically includes one or more surgeons, an anesthesiologist, and a nurse. Surgical techs help prepare the operating room before a surgery.

PUTTING YOUNG PATIENTS AT EASE

Going to a hospital or doctor's office for any reason can cause significant anxiety for young patients. That anxiety is magnified when any kind of testing is necessary. It's crucial that patients remain still for diagnostic imaging procedures such as X-rays or CT scans, but children have a hard time holding still when they are frightened. Medical equipment can be perceived as scary to kids, and imaging rooms are typically sterile, cold, and uninviting. One hospital in California set out to make imaging procedures worry-free experiences for children.

UCSF Benioff Children's Hospital has designed kid-friendly "scan suites." The suites are covered in colorful, themed murals and come complete with fun music, sound effects, and moving images projected to relax and entertain little patients. There are several imaging rooms, each with a unique theme. The latest addition is the hospital's Deep Blue Sea Adventure room, which features an MRI machine disguised as a submarine and projected images of turtles, otters, and fish for the patients to enjoy while being scanned. The new rooms are proving to be a big hit with their littlest patients. They are enabling radiologic techs to get clearer images and reducing the percentage of children who need antianxiety medication before a scan.

They are responsible for making sure all necessary equipment is where it should be. This includes sterile surgical instruments, medications, and supplies such as drapes, gowns, and gloves. They might help the surgeons put on their gowns and gloves or place surgical drapes on the patient before the procedure. The surgical technologist is trained to know the name and function of every surgical instrument, and during surgery, is called upon to quickly pass the surgeon instruments and other supplies. The surgical tech also has the important task of keeping a careful count of all instruments and supplies during the procedure so that nothing is left where it doesn't belong. The surgeon may remove tissue specimens that need to go to the lab. The surgical tech will pass these off to the circulating nurse. Some surgical tech functions are limited by state law or hospital policy. If allowed, surgical techs may complete tasks such as transporting patients to and from the operating room, shaving incision sites before surgery, and assisting in moving and positioning the patient on the surgical table. Surgical technicians who work in a hospital may have to work at all hours of the day and night, since emergencies that call for surgery can happen at any time. Those who work in a clinic that offers only elective surgeries will have a set work schedule since those surgeries are planned in advance.

The job outlook for future surgical technologists is promising. The BLS anticipates a faster-than-average 12 percent job growth rate between 2016 and 2026. An additional 12,600 jobs will be available to the surgical technologists of tomorrow.

A Career as a Radiologic Technologist

In order to become a radiologic technologist, students must complete two years or more of post-secondary education in an accredited program. Radiologic tech programs are offered by hospitals and at two- or four-year academic institutions. After successful completion of the program, candidates must pass a national certification examination. They must also complete continuing education hours in their field to remain registered as a radiologic technician.

Within radiologic technology, there are areas of specialization such as mammography, bone densitometry, magnetic resonance imaging, nuclear medicine, and sonography. Regardless of specialty area, all radiologic techs are medical personnel who are trained to perform diagnostic imaging procedures. Techs who specialize in radiation therapy are also trained to administer high doses of radiation to cancer patients. Radiologic techs have received a thorough education in anatomy, which is crucial when positioning a patient for a diagnostic imaging procedure. Patient safety is a top priority, and strict protocols must be followed to prevent exposure to radiation or injuries during a procedure. There are many methods of diagnostic imagery, such as X-rays, sound waves, CT scans, and magnetic resonance imaging. A radiologic tech may use one or more of them on a daily basis, depending on their place of work and their area of specialization. A typical workday for a radiologic technician involves taking images of several different patients, reviewing them for clarity, and consulting with the radiologist, as needed.

Radiologic techs enjoy fast-paced, interesting work environments, new patients, and the opportunity to gain valuable experience in many types of imaging technology.

Those interested in a career as a radiologic technologist can expect to see a fair amount of job growth in coming years. Between 2016 and 2026, the BLS predicts a 13 percent job growth rate. This will amount to more than thirty thousand new radiologic technologist positions.

Working as a Clinical Laboratory Technologist

Clinical laboratory technologists have earned a two-year associate's degree, at minimum. However, most

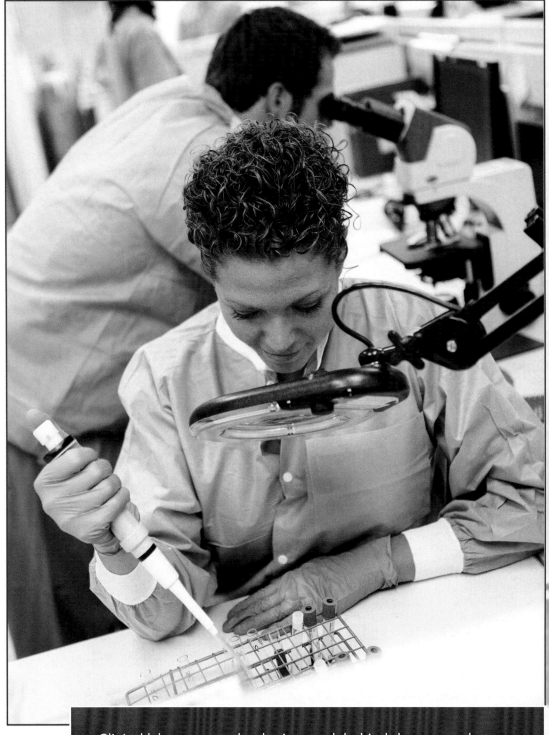

Clinical laboratory technologists work behind the scenes, but the role they play in medical care is vitally important to the health and well-being of patients.

applicants in this field have earned a bachelor's degree, and some possess graduate degrees. Landing a good job as a clinical lab tech is much more likely for those who have a bachelor's degree or other advanced degree. Many colleges offer undergraduate programs in clinical lab science. This is ideal, but another option is to earn a bachelor's degree in a natural science field, such as microbiology, and then enroll in a one-year program to earn a certificate in clinical lab science. Though not always required, some employers expect certification through the American Society for Clinical Pathology (ASCP). The American Medical Technologists (AMT) agency also offers medical technologist certification. There are a few states that require clinical lab techs to be licensed, and some health care professionals believe that will soon become the norm, so it's important to find out the necessary steps required by your state.

Clinical laboratory technologists are sometimes known as clinical laboratory scientists. Their job is to perform all laboratory tests. On any given day, they may receive samples from needle aspirations, cell scrapes, or blood draws. They use a microscope to view samples, and make detailed reports about their findings in each sample. If they discover an abnormality, they call in a doctor to confirm the abnormality and make the final diagnosis. If the sample is normal, with no abnormalities, laboratory technologists can document and report the normal findings without consulting a doctor. The majority of medical diagnoses are made based on laboratory test results, making laboratory technologists a crucial part of quality health care.

Doctors rely on laboratory technologists to help them make the right diagnosis.

Hundreds of thousands of people in the United States work as laboratory technologists, and there is a high demand for more of them in the workplace to help process samples more quickly and efficiently. According to the BLS, a job growth rate of 13 percent is expected for laboratory technologists between 2016 and 2026. This is faster-than-average growth and will result in 42,700 new jobs in this field over the next decade. This kind of job security gives peace of mind to many looking for jobs in the field of health care.

CHAPTER Five

Physical, Occupational, and Speech Therapists

Therapy can be defined as treatment intended to help heal an injury or relieve symptoms of a condition. Three prominent areas of specialization are physical therapy, occupational therapy, and speech therapy (more formally known as speech-language pathology). Professionals in these fields share the common goal of all health care professionals: improving the health and wellness of their patients.

A Career in Physical Therapy

Becoming a physical therapist (PT) requires a great deal of post-secondary education, with a heavy emphasis on life sciences. Programs are highly competitive and selective. Students considering a career as a physical therapist should take as many advanced science and health-related classes as possible in high school. Some colleges offer

Some physical therapists specialize in sports-related injuries, treating a variety of patients, from workout enthusiasts and players in recreational leagues to professional athletes.

a pre-physical therapy major. If that major is not offered, students can choose to major in a science, such as biology, exercise science, or kinesiology.

After completion of a bachelor's degree program, students will need to apply to an accredited academic doctor of physical therapy (DPT) degree program. Each program has its own criteria for admittance, so early research is important. Often, additional science courses are required that may not have been part of an applicant's bachelor's degree program. In addition to completing any specific prerequisites, applicants will need a high GPA and will need to take, and do well on, the Graduate Record Examination (GRE). DPT programs take a minimum of three years to complete and include rigorous coursework as well as practical experience in a supervised internship.

After successful completion of a DPT program, physical therapists need to be licensed to practice in their state. Each state has its own criteria for licensure, but every state requires candidates to pass the National Physical Therapy Examination (NPTE). Most states also require physical therapists to complete continuing education hours on an ongoing basis to keep their licensure current.

Many physical therapists practice in hospitals, but there are numerous other settings in which they also work. The majority of nursing or extended-care facilities and inpatient rehabilitation facilities have physical therapists on staff. Other places that utilize physical therapists include outpatient clinics, schools, hospices, and sports training facilities. Some physical therapists are in private practice and contract out to various facilities or even people's homes to provide care. Physical therapy clients include patients who have been in an accident and suffered injuries, those dealing with degenerative conditions, and those trying to manage chronic pain. Physical therapy provides a healthy alternative to addictive pain medications for those who live with chronic pain conditions such as fibromyalgia, osteoarthritis, and degenerative disc disease. Daily duties for physical therapists include assessing clients' needs based on their range of motion, level of pain, and severity of injury, developing individualized therapy programs, and working hands-on with clients as they complete their therapy regimen. Helping clients reach milestones in their recovery and reducing their levels of pain are two wonderful perks of working as a physical therapist.

The BLS expects the field of physical therapy to have a much-faster-than-average rate of job growth between 2016 and 2026, at 28 percent. There will be 67,100 new jobs in this booming industry. In large part, the increased demand for physical therapists can be attributed to an aging population that frequently requires rehabilitative services.

CHOOSING THE RIGHT GRADUATE SCHOOL

The cost of a program, its distance from home, and its reputation are all important factors in choosing a doctor of physical therapy program. With more than two hundred schools offering graduate programs for aspiring physical therapists, the choices can be overwhelming. Each program will have its own criteria and prerequisite courses, and those are also important factors in deciding which schools to consider. Perhaps one of the easiest factors to use in whittling down the list is that of reputation and ranking. In 2016, *U.S. News and World Report* ranked graduate physical therapy programs across the United States. Here are the top ten contenders and their locations:

University of Delaware in Newark, Delaware
University of Pittsburgh in Pittsburgh, Pennsylvania
University of Southern California in Los Angeles,
   California
Washington University in St. Louis, Missouri
Emory University in Atlanta, Georgia
Northwestern University in Chicago, Illinois
University of Iowa in Iowa City, Iowa
MGH Institute of Health Professions in Boston,
   Massachusetts
U.S. Army-Baylor University in Fort Sam Houston,
   Texas
Duke University in Durham, North Carolina

A Career in Occupational Therapy

As in the field of physical therapy, those interested
in becoming an occupational therapist (OT) have a
challenging academic path. Dual credit or advanced
classes in science that can be taken during high school
will help students get an early start on the years of
college coursework ahead. In college, most students
pursuing occupational therapy choose a science or
health-related major.

After completion of a bachelor's degree program,
students must apply to an accredited occupational therapy
program. This can be a master's level program—which
culminates in an MS, MA, MOT, or MSOT degree—or a
doctoral program, which awards either a DrOT or an OTD
degree. Students can expect to spend two to three years

Students interested in becoming a physical, occupational, or speech therapist complete many years of rigorous academic course work in pursuit of these rewarding careers.

in an occupational therapy master's program or a full three years for a doctoral program. Classroom learning and supervised experience in the field are both important parts of these programs. Those who choose a doctoral program also have a sixteen-week residency in a specific area of occupational therapy as part of their training.

Upon graduation from an occupational therapy program, candidates must apply for licensure in their state. Licensure is required for occupational therapists in every state, but other specific requirements vary from state to state. All occupational therapists are required to pass the National Board for Certification in Occupational Therapy (NBCOT) exam.

Occupational therapists work in hospitals, schools, nursing homes, and for in-home health services. They help people who have undergone a physical or mental trauma and lost some or all of their abilities to perform activities of daily living. Occupational therapists teach patients how to use adaptive equipment, when needed, and develop treatment plans to help them recover their abilities through a specific series of motions and exercises. They often work closely with other rehabilitative specialists such as physical therapists and speech-language pathologists. Successful occupational therapists are also excellent communicators with good interpersonal skills and a strong desire to help people.

According to a 2015 survey of occupational therapy graduates by the American Occupational Therapy Association, the vast majority of graduates received their first job offer in fewer than three months, and more than 80 percent of them found employment in their setting of choice. The BLS predicts continued good news for future occupational therapists. Between 2016 and 2026, the job growth rate will be 24 percent, with thirty-one thousand new jobs in the field.

A Career in Speech-Language Pathology

Speech-language pathologists (SLPs) also need an advanced degree to practice. High school students interested in this career should take advanced science

In a technique called articulation therapy, a speech therapist demonstrates how to form a sound and the patient uses a mirror to see if she is moving her mouth correctly.

courses, if possible, just like students interested in other therapy careers. Where available, internships or job shadowing are also very valuable to students wanting to preview the career and to be one step ahead before entering college.

A few colleges offer a bachelor's degree in speech-language pathology, but most do not. Students can major in a closely related field such as psychology, education, or American Sign Language. A high GPA is crucial to gaining acceptance into a graduate program. Upon completion of a bachelor's program, students can apply to an accredited speech-language pathology program. The Council on Academic Accreditation (CAA), a branch of the American Speech-Hearing-Language Association (ASHA), grants accreditation. ASHA is the governing body for all speech-language pathologists in the United States. Graduate SLP programs typically take two years to complete and include a clinical practicum consisting of 300 to 375 hours of supervised hands-on experience. Students must also pass the Educational Testing Service's Praxis exam in speech pathology and apply for licensure in the state where they wish to practice. Once a license is granted, they must complete a clinical fellowship year (CFY) to gain more hours of supervised experience. Finally, after completion of the fellowship year, candidates must take and pass the Certificate of Clinical Competency exam, at which time they are eligible for full licensure and certification as a speech-language pathologist.

Language-related difficulties can happen for many different reasons and to people of all ages, from infants to senior citizens. Speech-language pathologists are trained to help individuals overcome impairments and/or regain speech skills. Many patients seeing a speech-language pathologist have suffered a stroke or traumatic brain injury. Others may have been born with a hearing impairment or cleft palate. Some children need help working through developmental delays or overcoming a stutter or other speech problem. Speech-language pathologists evaluate, diagnose, and treat all of these conditions and more. They work in many different settings, including schools, hospitals, rehabilitation centers, long-term care facilities, doctors' offices, and in-home care.

Many school districts are experiencing a severe shortage of speech-language pathologists. This is largely due to the fact that school-based speech-language pathologists typically make much less than their colleagues who work in other settings. The job outlook for speech-language pathologists is very good. An 18 percent rate of job growth is expected between 2016 and 2026 according to the BLS. This will amount to 25,900 new jobs for those willing to put in the hard work and years of study required to enjoy this rewarding, challenging career.

CHAPTER Six

Careers in Mental Health

It goes without saying that mental health workers are excellent communicators with a passion for helping people. Individuals who pursue mental health careers are interested in connecting with people on a deep, meaningful level and seeing, firsthand, the positive impact one person can have on another. Students who are interested in psychology, enjoy working with people, and want to make a difference in their communities may find that a career in the field of mental health is a perfect fit. Psychiatrists, psychologists, and counselors are professionals who practice within the mental health field.

A Career as a Psychiatrist

Psychiatrists are mental health professionals who have achieved the highest level of education and training and successfully fulfilled the requirements of a doctoral program. As medical doctors, the job outlook for psychiatrists is included in the BLS entry for physicians, with the number of physician jobs expected to grow at a faster-than-average rate of 13 percent between 2016 and 2026. This equates to more than ninety thousand new jobs.

Mental health professionals must approach patients with great sensitivity and provide a comfortable setting where personal issues can be discussed in privacy.

After high school, the next step for students pursuing a career in psychiatry is to work toward a bachelor's degree with a major such as premed, psychology, biology, chemistry, or a related field. Sometime during their final year of undergraduate studies, students will need to take the Medical College Admission Test (MCAT) and apply to a medical school. A high GPA is required to gain admittance to medical school, as well as an impressive score on the MCAT.

Once admitted to a medical school program, students can expect two years of rigorous study in classrooms and labs, followed by two years of supervised work in hospitals and clinics, diagnosing and treating medical conditions. Psychiatry students complete clinical clerkships, treating patients with mental disorders. The goal of clerkships is for students to gain experience in five or more areas of psychiatric specialization.

After graduating from medical school, candidates must complete a four-year residency in psychiatry. During the first year, a resident will treat a variety of mental illnesses. In the remaining three years, the resident is trained in diagnosing mental illnesses and using a wide array of treatment methods under the supervision of experienced psychiatrists.

Like all doctors, psychiatrists need a license from their state's medical board to practice. After completing their four-year residency, the final requirement is for candidates to pass the required licensing test, as set forth by their state regulatory board. Many licensed psychiatrists also take the psychiatric certification exam to gain certification with the American Board of Psychiatry and Neurology (ABPN).

Psychiatrists see patients who have a wide variety of mental health concerns. During the consultation visit they get to know the patient and attempt to rule out any medical causes for mental health issues. Feelings of depression, anxiety, and mania are sometimes rooted in an underlying medical issue. If medical conditions are ruled out, the psychiatrist diagnoses the patient and comes up with a treatment plan for their specific mental health condition. An accurate diagnosis is crucial, as different conditions require completely different medications and therapies.

PSYCHIATRY: MYTHS AND MISCONCEPTIONS

There are those who sing the praises of psychiatrists, and others who remain skeptical and critical of the field. Here are a few common myths and misconceptions, according to Jennie Byrne, a psychiatrist with Cognitive Psychiatry of Chapel Hill:

1. **Psychiatrists think everyone has some sort of mental illness.** Actually, a diagnosis of mental illness is only reached when a person's behavior is so crippling they can no longer function in their daily lives as they previously have.

2. **Psychiatrists want all of their patients on medication.** Psychiatrists undergo years of advanced coursework, testing, and clinical experience to gain the knowledge they need to assess each patient on an individual basis and determine if medication would be helpful, or if it is unnecessary.

3. **Only "crazy" people need to see a psychiatrist.** The majority of patients seen by psychiatrists have very treatable illnesses or an imbalance that needs to be corrected.

4. **People who ask for help from psychiatrists are weak.** People who can acknowledge their limitations and reach out for help are actually very brave for doing so and should never be criticized.

5. **Any medical doctor can treat mental illness.** While medical doctors have an extensive

knowledge of the body, its systems, and treatment options for illnesses, they are not specifically trained to diagnose or treat any type of mental illness.

A Career as a Psychologist

Students interested in becoming psychologists should take any and all psychology courses they can in high school, including dual credit courses, to gain a head start in required coursework. After high school, students need to earn a bachelor's degree in psychology. The next step is an additional two years to obtain a master's degree in psychology, which qualifies psychologists to practice as caseworkers or social workers.

Those who wish to continue their education and become licensed clinical psychologists (LCPs) will enjoy more job opportunities and a higher salary. Obtaining a LCP certification requires completion of a doctoral program in psychology, which can take four to five years to complete. Most doctoral psychology programs include an internship that lasts up to two thousand hours. Most doctoral programs also offer a postdoctoral fellowship program. Fellowship programs typically take a year to complete and allow students to gain supervised work experience.

In order to practice independently, clinical psychologists must be licensed. Most states require applicants to have passing scores on the Examination for Professional Practice in Psychology, as well as successful

Typically, mental health professionals will assess a patient in the initial consultation, with follow-up appointments tailored to meet the patient's individual needs.

completion of a doctoral program, internship, and at least one year of professional experience. After licensure, most states also require LCPs to complete continuing education hours to maintain their licenses.

Psychologists are experts in human behavior. Their professional objective is to help patients overcome emotional or psychological difficulties. Psychologists work in schools, doctors' offices, health clinics, community centers, hospitals, nursing facilities, and in government-funded programs. Psychologists may also work for private corporations interested in improving employee productivity or job satisfaction. Depending on the work environment, daily duties for a psychologist may consist of meeting with clients individually or in groups, assessing problems and devising plans to solve them, and providing mental health support and encouragement to clients facing mental health issues.

The BLS predicts a faster-than-average increase of 14 percent in job growth between 2016 and 2026. This equates to twenty-three thousand new jobs for psychologists during that time frame. As with other health care professions, the job outlook is encouraging for future psychologists.

A Career as a Counselor

Counselors are mental health professionals who have completed advanced coursework and training to gain the knowledge and skills to help people struggling with a variety of problems. High school students interested in a counseling career should take classes such as psychology, humanities, and sociology, if available. Talking with a school counselor about the field is also a great opportunity to learn more.

After high school, earning a bachelor's degree is the next step. A major in psychology or a closely related field is recommended. Some students interested in being school counselors choose to major in education. Maintaining a high GPA is important, as is any volunteer or work experience that is related to a student's major. Upon completion of a bachelor's degree program, students should continue their educations with a graduate degree program in counseling, which typically takes two to three years to complete. Graduate programs teach students to diagnose and treat a variety of conditions. Licensure is required in all states for counselors to practice. The licensed practicing counselor (LPC) certification is the most common, but some areas of specialty in counseling award their own unique license. Supervised clinical experience totaling at least two thousand hours is required before licensure, and candidates must also pass a national board exam.

All counselors meet with clients on a regular basis, first to assess their needs and then to provide individualized therapy. There are many different specialty areas within counseling, including mental health counseling, marriage and family counseling, school counseling, and substance abuse counseling. Counselors offer guidance and psychological and emotional support. Effective counselors are compassionate and committed to helping people. With the help of a good counselor, many people replace harmful coping mechanisms with safe ones, learn to make better choices for themselves, gain self-confidence, and move toward healthier, happier relationships.

The current shortage of mental health professionals and projected increase in demand means students pursuing these careers can look forward to excellent pay and job stability.

The job outlook for students wishing to pursue any type of mental health profession is encouraging. The BLS predicts a 23 percent growth rate for jobs in counseling between 2016 and 2026. This means a total of 60,300 new jobs in counseling will be added between 2016 and 2026.

CHAPTER Seven

Pursuing a Fulfilling Career

There are so many jobs in health services that choosing just the right career path is a big decision. Entry-level experience in any area of health care is a great starting point, regardless of long-range goals. After academic requirements have been met and the necessary skills and experience for the position accrued, the job search process begins. Making the most of job search resources and thoroughly preparing for each interview are the last hurdles to landing the perfect job.

The Job Search

There are many free online resources available to job seekers. Each site features different search tools, allowing the user to narrow the search. Some of the most user-friendly sites allow users to search according to location, employer, job skills, or job title. Job search sites number in the hundreds, and job seekers will first need to choose which ones to use. Some of the most popular job sites include Indeed, CareerBuilder, Dice, Glassdoor, Idealist, LinkedIn, Monster, US.jobs, Google for Jobs, and LinkUp. Employers don't list job openings on every site, so job seekers should utilize several job search

Job search sites are just one of several options available to job seekers and should be used in conjunction with other strategies, such as social networking and attending job fairs.

sites to have the best chance of seeing all relevant postings. There are also sites, such as Hired or Simply Hired, that are designed to let job seekers take a more active role, posting their own specific requirements as well as qualifications. These sites allow users to avoid unwanted emails about jobs that don't fit their requirements. Local job fairs are excellent options for job seekers as well. They are usually free to attend, and there are job fairs that specifically showcase careers in health care. Attendees have the opportunity to speak with representatives from many different departments or companies, and often can submit applications and résumés during the event. Sometimes applicants can interview during these events, too. Attendees should dress as if they are going to an interview and have hard copies of their résumés in hand.

Most people now have some kind of online presence. Social media platforms such as Facebook, Instagram, and Twitter are some of the most popular and can be helpful for networking with others to spread the word when job searching. They can also be a good way to learn more about companies and organizations that are of interest. Personal posts including pictures, comments, and updates are typical fare, but it's important to remember that people other than family and friends may see the posts. It's common practice for employers to look up applicants on the Net. Privacy settings are helpful to safeguard personal posts, but careful consideration of content is essential. An unprofessional, unflattering online presence may prevent hiring managers from reaching out.

The Interview Process

After finding one or more positions to apply for, it's important to have a professional, polished résumé. Care should be taken to ensure there are no typos, grammatical errors, or misspellings. Job skills and accomplishments should be highlighted in short bullet points, making the résumé streamlined and easy to read. Hiring managers are likely to just skim over résumés that are written with long sentences and blocks of text.

TIPS FOR A SUCCESSFUL INTERVIEW

Daunting though they may be, interviews are an essential step in landing a good job. Applicants need to let their true personalities shine through, showcasing their strengths and projecting confidence without sounding rehearsed. Depending on the position an applicant is pursuing, preparation for interviews will vary somewhat, but there are tried-and-true tips that experts agree will increase the likelihood of having a successful interview.

1. Practice before the interview.
2. Thoroughly research the company or organization ahead of time.
3. Dress for success in a clean, crisp outfit.
4. Arrive at least five minutes ahead of the scheduled interview time.
5. Try to remain calm and relaxed.
6. Be friendly and courteous to all staff members.
7. Remember to use positive body language, such as smiling, making eye contact, sitting up straight, and actively listening.
8. Fully engage in the interview, asking questions as well as answering them.
9. Give specific examples that highlight relevant experience, job skills, and accomplishments.
10. Show enthusiasm and appreciation, thanking the interviewer for his or her time.

The next step is to prepare for the interview process by watching mock interviews, reviewing common interview questions, and holding a practice interview with a friend or family member playing the role of hiring manager and giving constructive feedback. Common interview questions include:

> Why are you interested in this position?
> What are your greatest strengths/weaknesses?
> Why do you feel you're a good fit for this position?
> What are your long-term career goals?
> If hired, when are you available to start?

Going through more than one practice interview is especially helpful, varying the questions and "hiring manager" each time. An outfit that is wrinkle and stain-free should be picked out ahead of time and worn during the practice interviews as well.

Reaching out to the hiring manager after the interview is a professional courtesy. It shows an applicant is appreciative of the opportunity to interview, enthusiastic about the company, driven, and thoughtful. This can be done through email or a note can be hand-delivered to the office. As an added bonus, following up after the interview is another opportunity for applicants to get their names in front of the hiring manager one more time before a decision is made.

Properly preparing for an interview gives applicants a boost of confidence and tips the scales in favor of a successful interview. Advancement is common within the health services industry, and the skills gained in entry-level positions are essential for ambitious people who want to climb the ladder in a fulfilling job where they can help people every day. The field of health services is

Interviewees who are qualified, prepared, dressed professionally, and who show a genuine interest in the company or organization stand a good chance of quickly landing a job.

growing at a tremendous pace. There are positions for those with a degree from technical schools, two- or four-year colleges, and of course those who have advanced degrees. There are also some entry-level positions for high school graduates that provide on-the-job training. The high demand for well-qualified employees in the health services industry means those who are willing to complete the necessary educational requirements and hours of training are likely to enjoy a very rewarding long-term career with many opportunities for growth.

ANESTHESIOLOGIST A professional trained in sedating patients through the use of medicines called anesthetics.

ANXIETY An uneasy, nervous, uncertain feeling about an upcoming event.

AUTONOMY The freedom to work independently, without supervision.

GRADUATE RECORD EXAMINATION (GRE) A standardized test that is required for admittance by most graduate schools in the United States.

MANUAL DEXTERITY The ability to move one's hands and fingers skillfully and manipulate objects with precise movements.

MEDICAID A government program that helps cover medical costs for low-income individuals.

MEDICARE A federal health insurance program for individuals over the age of sixty-five.

MICROBIOLOGY A branch of science that deals specifically with microorganisms.

NEEDLE ASPIRATION A procedure in which a hollow needle is inserted into a lump to remove a sample of cells to be examined under a microscope.

NONPROFITS Organizations that are formed and that operate without making a profit.

ORTHODONTICS The treatment of misalignments and malformations in the teeth, often using braces to correct the problem.

PERIODONTICS An area of dentistry that focuses on the tissues and structures surrounding and supporting the teeth.

PHARMACOLOGY The branch of medicine that revolves around the use and effects of different drugs in treating patients.

RADIOLOGIST A medical professional trained to read and interpret diagnostic images such as X-rays.

RESIDENCY In medicine, the period of time a graduate student is working under the supervision of licensed practitioners to gain experience.

RIGOROUS Extremely thorough, demanding, and challenging.

SUPPLEMENTAL Something provided in addition to what is already available.

TERMINAL In medicine, a condition that is incurable and will lead to death.

UNDERGRADUATE A college student who is working on, but has not yet earned, a bachelor's degree.

VACCINATIONS A medical treatment administered to give the patient immunity to a certain disease, such as measles.

For More Information

American Occupational Therapy Association, Inc. (AOTA)
4720 Montgomery Lane
Bethesda, MD 20814
(301) 652-6611
Website: https://www.aota.org
Facebook: @AmericanOccupationalTherapyAssociationAOTA
Twitter: @AOTAinc
The American Occupational Therapy Association is a
    professional association established in 1917. Its goal
    is to advance the quality, availability, and support of
    occupational therapy. This website offers in-depth
    information about education, careers, and events in the
    field of occupational therapy.

American Physical Therapy Association (APTA)
1111 North Fairfax Street
Alexandria, VA 22314-1488
(703) 684-7343
Website: https://www.apta.org
Facebook: @AmericanPhysicalTherapyAssociation
Twitter: @aptatweets
The American Physical Therapy Association is an
    organization for students and professionals in the field
    of physical therapy. This website offers information
    about education and careers in physical therapy and
    the latest news in the industry.

American Speech-Language-Hearing Association (ASHA)
2200 Research Blvd.
Rockville, MD 20850
(800) 638-8255
Website: https://www.asha.org

Facebook: @asha.org

Twitter: @ASHAWeb

This website offers information about the fields of speech-language pathology and audiology for students and professionals, including the latest career and practice management information.

HOSA-Future Health Professionals

548 Silicon Drive, Suite 101

Southlake, TX 76092

(800) 321-HOSA

Website: http://www.hosa.org

Facebook: @hosafhp

Twitter: @NationalHOSA

HOSA-Future Health Professionals is an organization for high school and college students pursuing careers in the health profession. This website includes information on membership, events, scholarships, and resources for students.

National Academy of Future Physicians

1701 Pennsylvania Avenue NW, Suite 200

Washington, DC 20006

(617) 307-7425

Website: https://www.futuredocs.com

Facebook and Twitter: @futuredocsnow

This website offers prospective medical students information about leadership training and their academy programs. Their goal is to encourage more students to pursue medical careers.

Nursing the Future
1517 Ewart Avenue
Saskatoon, Saskatchewan S7H 2K7
Canada
Website: http://www.nursingthefuture.ca
Email:newgraduates@nursingthefuture.ca
Twitter: @Ntfnewgraduates
Nursing the Future is a Canadian organization that offers
    mentorships to new graduates of nursing programs.
    This website includes helpful links and a blog with
    relevant information about the field of nursing.

Speech-Language & Audiology Canada
1000-1 Nicholas Street
Ottawa ON K1N 7B7
Canada
(800) 259-8519
Website: https://www.sac-oac.ca
Twitter: @sac_oac
This Canadian organization supports and promotes
    speech-language and audiology careers. Their website
    offers information, resources, and the latest news in
    the industry.

For Further Reading

Brezina, Corona. *Getting a Job in Health Care.* New York, NY: Rosen Publishing, 2014.

Byers, Ann. *Jump-Starting a Career in Dietetics & Nutrition.* New York, NY: Rosen Publishing, 2014.

Colbert, Bruce J., and Elizabeth D. Katrancha. *Career Success in Health Care: Professionalism in Action.* Boston, MA: Cengage Learning, 2015.

Culp, Jennifer. *Jump-Starting Careers as Medical Assistants & Certified Nursing Assistants.* New York, NY: Rosen Publishing, 2014.

Goldberg, Edward M. *So, You Want to Be a Physician: Getting an Edge in the Pursuit of Becoming a Physician or Other Medical Professional.* North Charleston, SC: CreateSpace, 2018.

Hubbard, Rita. *What Degree Do I Need to Pursue a Career in Health Care?* New York, NY: Rosen Publishing, 2015.

Hunsaker, Jennifer. *Physical Therapists* (Careers in Healthcare). Broomall, PA: Mason Crest, 2017.

Leavitt, Amie. *Jump-Starting a Career in Medical Technology.* New York, NY: Rosen Publishing, 2014.

Lusted, Marcia Amidon. *Jump-Starting a Career in Physical Therapy & Rehabilitation.* New York, NY: Rosen Publishing, 2014.

Sack, Rebekah. *The Young Adult's Survival Guide to Interviews: Finding the Job and Nailing the Interview.* Ocala, FL: Atlantic Publishing Group, 2016.

Sternberg, Robert J. *Career Paths in Psychology: Where Your Degree Can Take You.* Washington, DC: American Psychological Association, 2016.

Bibliography

Association of American Medical Colleges. "Medical Specialties - Explore Options - Choose Your Specialty - Careers In Medicine." February 3, 2018. http://www.aamc.org/cim/specialty/exploreoptions/list.

Doyle, Alison. "7 Interview Tips That Will Help You Get the Job." The Balance Careers, December 13, 2017. http://www.thebalance.com/top-interview-tips-2058577.

ExploreHealthCareers.org. "Surgical Technologist." January 25, 2018. http://www.explorehealthcareers.org/career/allied-health-professions/surgical-technologist.

FOX2now.com, St. Louis. "Physical Therapy Eases Pain, Provides Alternative to Opioids." February 19, 2018. http://fox2now.com/2018/02/19/physical-therapy-eases-pain-provides-alternative-to-opioids.

Gask, Linda. "I'm a Psychiatrist-and I Live With Depression." *Psychiatric Times*, January 21, 2016. http://www.psychiatrictimes.com/depression/im-psychiatristand-i-live-depression.

Goldenberg Matt. "How a Psychiatrist Treats Depression: A Peek Behind the Curtain." Huffington Post, December 1, 2014. http://www.huffingtonpost.com/dr-matt-goldenberg-do-/how-a-psychiatrist-treats_b_6244256.html.

Grant, Rebecca. "The U.S. Is Running Out of Nurses." *The Atlantic*, February 3, 2016. http://www.theatlantic.com/health/archive/2016/02/nursing-shortage/459741.

Hardiman, Samuel. "TPS Forced to Cope with Speech Language Pathologist Shortage." *Tulsa World*, November 28, 2017. http://www.tulsaworld.com/news/tps-forced-to-cope-with-speech-language-pathologist-shortage/article_97b891ec-b96b-566d-87f7-1123423c0d93.html.

McKay, Dawn Rosenberg. "Get the Facts About Being an RN." The Balance Careers, January 31, 2017. http://www.thebalance.com/registered-nurse-526062.

Mclean-Green, Keisha. "5 Ways Substance Abuse Counselors Make a Difference." Absolute Advocacy, March 13, 2016. http://www.absoluteadvocacy.org/5-ways-substance-abuse-counselors-make-difference.

Morris, Sylvia. "Get to Know a Day in the Life Hospitalist." *U.S. News and World Report*, September 2, 2014. http://www.usnews.com/education/blogs/medical-school-admissions-doctor/2014/09/01/get-to-know-a-day-in-the-life-of-a-hospitalist+.

Public Broadcasting Service (PBS). "PBS--Healthcare Crisis: Healthcare Timeline." February 10, 2018. http://www.pbs.org/healthcarecrisis/history.htm.

Reshwan, Robin. "5 Expert Tips for Interview Success." *U.S. News & World Report*, June 19, 2017. http://money.usnews.com/money/blogs/outside-voices-careers/articles/2017-06-19/5-expert-tips-for-interview-success+.

Santiago, Andrea Clement. "What Is Therapy? What Are Therapy Careers?" Verywell Health, May 8, 2017. http://www.verywell.com/types-of-therapy-careers-in-healthcare-1736198.

Teach: Make a Difference. "How to Become a Speech-Language Pathologist." January 1, 2018. http://www.teach.com/become/other-education-careers/school-speech-language-pathologist.

Thompson, Derek. "Health Care Just Became the U.S.'s Largest Employer." *The Atlantic*, January 9, 2018.

http://www.theatlantic.com/business/archive/2018/01 /health-care-america-jobs/550079.

UCSF Radiology. "Patient-Friendly Pediatric Scan Suites Ease 'Scanxiety.'" November 23, 2016. http://radiology .ucsf.edu/blog/patient-friendly-pediatric-scan-suites -ease-%E2%80%9Cscanxiety%E2%80%9D.

U.S. News & World Report. "2017 Best Graduate Physical Therapy Programs | US News Rankings." Retrieved February 8, 2018. http://www.usnews.com/best -graduate-schools/top-health-schools/physical -therapy-rankings/page+2.

U.S. News and World Report. "Community Health Worker Ranks Among Best Jobs of 2018." January 28, 2018. http://money.usnews.com/careers/best-jobs /community-health-worker.

U.S. News and World Report. "What Is a Community Health Worker?" Best Jobs U.S. News Rankings. February 10, 2018. https://money.usnews.com/careers /best-jobs/community-health-worker.

Weakley, Lizzie. "5 Good Reasons to Become a Nurse." Health ECareers, December 7, 2015. http://www .healthecareers.com/article/career/reasons-to-become -a-nurse.

Index

About the Author

Jessica Shaw has a BA in psychology from Texas State University. She has worked in human services and taught preschool, and she currently writes nonfiction, fiction, and poetry for children and young adults, including standardized testing material and work appearing in numerous children's publications.

Photo Credits